FINISHING LINE PRESS

www.finishinglinepress.com

CHOOSING A STONE

poems by

Richard Hedderman

Finishing Line Press
Georgetown, Kentucky

CHOOSING A STONE

Special thanks to Robin Mello, Joan Williamson, Nancy Takacs, Richard
Foerster, Karla Huston, Mary Kate Hedderman, Peter Cameron-Gilsey, and
Judith Kerman and all the poets at the 2017 Mayapple Writers Retreat in
Woodstock, NY for their invaluable critique.

Publisher: Leah Maines
Editor: Christen Kincaid
Cover Art: elnavegante/Shutterstock.com
Author Photo: Darren Hauck
Cover Design: Elizabeth Maines McCleavy

Printed in the USA on acid-free paper.
Order online: www.finishinglinepress.com
             also available on amazon.com

Author inquiries and mail orders:
Finishing Line Press
P. O. Box 1626
Georgetown, Kentucky 40324
U. S. A.

Table of Contents

PART III

For Robin

"Midstream he halted again and slid the bow from his shoulder and let it go in the river. It turned and jostled in the riffles and floated out into the pool below. A crescent of pale wood, turning and drifting, lost in the sun on the water. Legacy of some drowned archer, musician, maker of fire."

Cormac McCarthy, *The Crossing*

"I no longer stand helpless before nature."

Vincent van Gogh to Theo van Gogh,
Etten, Holland, September 1881

"As for man, his days are as grass;
as a flower of the field, so he flourisheth.

For the wind passeth over it, and it is gone;
and the place thereof shall know it no more."

Psalm 103, 15-16

PART I

DUSK

In the great blue
spruce bats hang
like live coals.

A DRIFTWOOD FIRE IN WINTER

This is what I promised you: a driftwood fire in winter.
So when dusk plunged the cove into shadow,
and the tides dragged evening ashore,

I cobbled bundles of sea-strewn wreckage
from the stony beach and lugged them back:
the salt-bleached bones of spruce and oak,

shards of lobster trap, the broken ribs of ketch
and trawler, splinters of spar and yawl,
stem, sprit and keel—the wrack

of a continent sundered and driven shoreward
in the Atlantic's mythic pound. What the seas
tossed up, I gathered for us and hauled home.

So, we travel far tonight, my dear mariner,
on this raft of sea-smoke, before this driftwood
fire of our making, the one I built for you.

Then let me stroke your hair as we moor
in love's familiar harbor watching together
as the smoke of our blaze unfurls.

STEELHEAD

When it rips the surface,
the thick tail shudders,
with a brazen slash
salutes the greensward
and the roll of the hills
and smacks the new untried air.

The fish, armed now with the gun-metal
tang of blood in the mouth, charged
with the hook's voltage,
arcs into the day's blue tropic,
oxygen scorching its gills.

The fisherman foam-flecked and agog,
takes in the marvelous heft and shine,
the unknowable flare of the jaw,
the flint of the eye.

The river is poised now to collect the fish
and grow quiet again,
the air standing around it in fathoms

as it staves off the sky's clutch,
the pull of the world,
and descends.

HAMMOCK SEASON

Hawsered in this languorous snare,
I'm lolling in summer's blue estuaries,
breaking the sky's miraculous
code under the eyelid's revenant eclipse
where July's fireworks flower.

Indolence is the virtue
of those suspended, slumped
in the sag of slumber. How easily
my vocabulary yields to the z's of idleness:
doze, daze, drowse and laze.

I've grown the pelt of the sloth
and can no longer grasp
the yard rake or the hoe.
Let the compost go unturned,
the grass become deep as a bed.

Let the employable and the conscientious
bustle and fuss. I'm weightless with the gods
of the sun, nodding like a sunflower in the breeze.
And when the Muse arrives, tell her
to come back when I'm not so busy.

This is going to take awhile.

THE GREAT HORNED OWL'S MONOLOGUE

Daylight scarred the water. Scalded in afternoon's
fiery cauldron, I retreated into the timber, spurs

stropped on the thin air. Now I trawl the shadows,
eternity's insomniac, implacable executioner

to the blundering vole, the inconsequential mice.
In the light of jagged moons I pluck the meek

and the foolish, asking my insoluble questions,
claws poised for a wrong answer. My spoils bleed.

Bones lowered from the beak's meat hook
improve my midden. Neck swiveling, obdurate sockets

sweeping the horizon, every twitch snugged
in the eye's yellow noose. When the naked hare blinks,

I gather the small ghost of its heart into my talons.
The snow is just killing time. My mask is calm.

In my icy hood I hear everything.
The red star bruises my shoulder.

THE DISCOVERY OF HEAVEN

Even beforehand the questions started:
How many angels? How many reincarnations?

Only the one God? Where
is the afterlife? How about potatoes?

Coffee? Are there green vales and good pasture?
Boogie-woogie piano?

Was it somewhere to go, like smoke,
when you drifted up through sleep?

One day, martins darted on high winds
in the blue void between two sudden worlds,

incomprehensible, without measure.
Then heaven became a place

to lie down in for an hour,
with the long summer sun on our faces,

amid the drone of bees in a tended garden,
and above us the vitreous savannas of cloud.

OPHELIA

Under spring stars,
he touched my face and breasts
and the innumerable moons of my body.

For months, I listened for him
everywhere, hearing his laugh now and again
down stone corridors or across the hushed drifts
that chilled Elsinore.

And once only did I find him,
that shadow darkening his strange brow
talking to the players in whispers
in a cold chamber.

My refuge, then, was the childhood willow
where I climbed and sang clear
above the brook.

And when I descended into the arms
of the water, I turned slowly
listening with eyelashes, fingertips,
one arm thrown out to the current
that swallowed me like snow.

THE INVADERS

Their crest is a raven
perched on a dead branch.
Smoke from a besieged city
their tattered flag.

Drained by pillage and ambuscades,
all invaders finally are the same:
exhausted, bloodied, far from the sea.

Navigating by stars already burned out,
and following the branches of snow
into evening.

Plundered villages burn
under the north star.

And as the wind sweeps their tracks,
a wounded captain stands in the snow,
a broken compass held to his ear
like a shell.

READING BEOWULF

—Dimond Library, University of New Hampshire

1. *Approaching the Danish Coast*

At first light, land emerged—
a shade deeper than the sea
and aching with the silence
of a plundered church.

When the crew hailed land
I came to the rail and saw him,
one of Hrothgar's men,
posted on the shore and forgotten.
Straddling a shaggy horse, he waited
on the immaculate neck of beach.

He was like any sentry: nervous,
swathed in hides, grimed fingers on the reins.
A ghost the wind had changed to stone.

He knew nothing of us,
nothing of cordage or tides
or navigating the ice-mists
of the whale-road.

My men, their lashes snowed with salt,
were suddenly hushed in the off-shore smell
of wood smoke and bogs.

I waited for him to speak.
I stood alone
in the listening prow
too brave for weapons
and my eyes blue as a hurricane.

2. *Arrival at Heorot*

We rose from the sea,
from the plain of the dead
toward that hall that once
illumined the north.

Our marching wakened the foreland.
The heath trembled, the sky
a mirror of the unbroken sea
we had just crossed.

Rain. It had always rained.
The earth was mired, bloodied
as every pond and puddle
reflected our passing.

Hrothgar's people eyed us
from dark cloaks steeped in rain.

We heard their voices
in the long grass,
in the unrelieved mourning
of the wind.

Our armor rattled, scattering them:
waxed spear-shafts, shields
and bright boar-helms
hauled across the moor.

Bronze blazed our helmets
in the skein of morning.

3. *Grendel*

The moon hung like a boar's tusk
in a night sky spilled from an ink-horn.

We slept in our armor

in the cold light of the hall-glow;
but nobody really slept.

I'd wanted him in daylight,
in the fever of noon,
and had no use for night
with its sweats and chills.

As the moon tipped its horns,
he came over the moors, mist-walker,
shadow-thief, hoarder of dead souls,
trailing the smell of fen-bottoms and wolf blood.

He stood in the doorway
soaking up the starlight like a mountainside,
fur smoldering, his yellow eyes
flickering like torches in the wind.

He seized one of my men and devoured him
whole, head first like a plucked fowl
as I waited and watched, gathering
the power of the dead.

And when I closed with him,
we grappled and rolled, toppling mead-benches
and scattering the King's flagons.

I clutched an arm and tore
where the rivers of blood
forked in his body,
where the roots of his flesh diverged.

The limb pulled loose and my throat seized
in the raw stink of blood;
his howl unhinged doors the size of mead-tables
and he bolted, wailing, into the night.

I slung the still-quivering arm
across stag antlers pegged over the throne
where it hung, drained of gore,
the blood-spout stopped.

4. *At the Mere*

They led me up gnarled goat-trails
toward the lair of the fen-mother,
past steaming bogholes of black storm-water.

I preferred the sea, where danger
was the violet smudge of a waterspout
glimpsed on the horizon, or the war-field
and a turret of thick smoke
rising beyond the next hill.

I thought back on the flatlands of home,
of streams in the hard glint of sun;
armor, weapons revealed
in caches after the first thaw.

This was different; nothing moved.
Only the clouds frothed and churned.
No one spoke. It drizzled,
soaking the heath-floor.

A deer hoof disturbed
a coil of fog.

5. *Hrothgar to Beowulf*

In my time, I saw crops rise
warrior-thick and maidens,
their ropes of hair shining;
stallions set off in blue mist.

Now there is only sadness in the depth
of the harp. In its throbbing,
the wail of a thousand warriors
dead under my command whose flames
the candle no longer sustains.

The stamp of a hoof in the courtyard—
sharp memory.

I am old now, I sense it
in the odor of smoke at dusk.

Why do the grasses
grow so long in summer?

I will die, Beowulf, and so will you
in your turn. They will find me
one morning on a bench by the hearth,
a bowl of milk in my lap,
women sweeping around me.

But you, let your blood spill
when it is time, that its flowing
like the blast of a battle-horn
may sustain the pride that drives you.

For know this, Beowulf:
Age gathers together fragments of time;
the grasses that grow so long
are finally whitened by snow.

6. *The Dragon*

In a flame-hollowed chamber of stone,
he had slept away the drizzling centuries
perched on a throne of soft-hued metals
like a sundial at midnight.

He smoldered, waiting for the ages to pass,
for moss to grow again on blood-stained
altars of ice-cracked stone,
for the stars to once again
grind their dust into snow, for the sun
to fall back into its molten lake
at the rim of the world.

Then came the winter of the dragon.
And in the earth-dark of the barrow,
his scales began to shine
like the obsidian that night is mined from.

And then I was standing
in a shadowless noon, watching
as he raised his battle flags—
the flame-torn roof of my hall.

I knew then that I would have to embrace him
like a smell, like heat and pain,
that somehow we were alike
as two chimes from a bell,
that my pride would be repaid with fire.

When my shield had blistered and burned,
and I was scorched under the burning wind
of his anger I knew, as pain
swirled in the wound,
that I would break free of my own shadow.

I knew that I would unravel the flesh-knot
and sleep on the funeral pyre,
that my heart would float
on its stem of smoke.

That the sky would cradle me.

BIRCHES

i
Does the mind travel back
to those bonewhite limbs? Locked
in memory the sound
of white trunks
swaying at night.

ii
I saw birches
loosen in the fog.
Old silk
Chinese drawings
unfolded.

iii
On a cold morning,
birches awoken.
Around them were built
strong houses of daylight.

iv
Cold winter morning.
The forest so crisp
I could hear it. Birches
around a deep lake
throwing shadows.

v
I would choose: drown
in that whiteness, or
take hold of a living branch,
and for a while be pulled back
into the quiet roots of my life.

HORSE LESSONS

—for M.B. and Bastion

In late afternoon light,
I'd watched him round the paddock,
sweeping closer with each pass—
a river of prairie wind.
Dust was everywhere.
green dust of alfalfa, ancient dust
of horses, floating in spears
of sunlight just beyond the cool dark
of the barn. I'd learned
the lesson of the cross-ties—
not to cross behind—and never again
to lean on the electric fence.
I'd learned to groom him,
to work slowly from head to tail,
keeping the curry comb moving
in tight, vigorous circles. That day,
as I worked the comb,
his coat flowed and rippled under my hand,
as the roots of my own muscles
began to ache and shudder.
He grew still. The great, brown muzzle
dipped toward earth,
eyes bright with power
as I brushed clouds
from his astonished coat.
All at once, I seemed aware
of everything: the infinite strokes
of the comb, smell of hide and hay,
the weight of horses, long evening skies,
the bliss of summer grasses,
and imagined he would ascend
and ride the perfect air. I spoke
as I brushed, though I knew
I didn't have to, repeating his name
like a spell into an ear

that twitched with recognition:
Bastion, Bastion, Bastion.

AT NIGHT

When I reach out at night
with my one, orphaned foot
lost on the sheet's snowbound prairie,
looking for you, and touch
the sole of your foot

nestled in sleep,
I touch the part of you farthest
from me.

You mutter irritably and stir,
the blankets rustling
like a sudden bolt of rain
in night trees.

And when you push my foot
back, it's like a shove off
from the shore of sleep

where I drift, once more alone,
down the bed's long dark stream.

READING YOURSELF TO SLEEP

Eyelids flutter over the blank verse
of sleep. You brush the crow's wings

from your face. The book, perhaps a collection
of Chekhov's short stories, spills

from your hands and tumbles into the dark
as through still water, sinking

under the weight of words. You follow,
flumed like a spent swimmer,

happy for the long, quiet slide
into the book's depths

and down into the dark's feathery river.
The full moon, like the Pequod's coin

weights your eyelids. Regret streams away
through the countless estuaries

of sentences until you finally let go.
Go ahead. The page numbers

will mark the way. The chapters
will toll the fathoms.

Part II

FIRST DAY OF SPRING

I washed my hands in snow
and dried them
on a blue shirt.

CHOOSING A STONE I

Go out and gather stones
when it's raining,
on a day when a single gesture

anchors the world and a stone
reflects the deeper contemplation
of whoever cradles it,

shining and wet in his palm.
Its silence is of men
who have fished too long,

of hunters who return home
through bare trees.
Lover of animals, namer of stars,

choose a stone, dense with the weight
of an unanswered question.
Plunge it into a lake

where the dark surface
has been smoothed by cold.
The world shudders in its absence

which the widening rings
quietly confirm.

BASQUE COOKING

Plenty of potatoes, garlic and lamb.
Bundles of sage and jugs of harsh red wine.
Spring trout, the iridescent flanks
poached to a flaky pink.

Heels of dark bread with pig feet soup.
Fiddle head ferns
fried in olive oil and thyme.
There's stewed rabbit with tomatoes,

and toasted sheep's milk cheese.
Mutton with white beans and parsley
simmered over an oak fire—in nearly everything
the savor of wood smoke, even in the luminous,

black-eyed prawns *a la plancha*
bristling with salt.

CLOUDS

Sometime, just watch the sky-map
of cloud drift over the trees
or down the length of a pond.
How easily the sky gathers its terrain
crossed by valleys and roads.

Watch carefully for the countries:
a map of Japan or a Norse land,
its chilly borders shaded with firs,
its earth churned by a flying horse.

Yesterday, I lay back
against the forest floor
and watched as they went past,
those water-colored galleons
of the east, their sails dragging.

They made the aspens rattle,
the quaking leaves remembered
their passing,
and I knew then what it was
to stretch out in silk, in umber.

COAT OF ARMS

Choose from among them,
that would be my way,
for there are as many as dead in a cemetery:

a full moon, its flags burning;
a regiment of defeated crusaders
retreating across a dark field,

or naked lovers, their fists in each other's hair;
a naturalist with sheepdog and scythe;
some armaments and a drum;

a wide, shallow bowl of red fruit,
before a querulous maiden, her hair
about to catch fire.

Then there's the tall window of thick glass,
stained by crushed hawthorns
and the end of the day.

A few pale stars wink out
over the horizon where a dream
uncoils and waits. Revenge

sweetens the sky. In my favorite,
there's no fountain or orchard
in sight, no sheaf of barley,

just a clutch of fiery roses and a scarlet wound
where the family name was torn away
to make a headstone.

THE FIRST PLAYER'S MONOLOGUE

We will use all gently, my lord,
even the darkness that englobes
the fluttering soul of each candle.
We will wait for your signal—
standing on a coffin lid,
sawing the air with both hands
and begin at the raven's first,
querulous cry, long after twilight
has cleared the ramparts. Soon,
we will find ourselves once again
in the garden, where sooner or later
we all come to ruin, and will orchestrate
your disharmony: this play about poison
and torches, the malevolence of power
and the evil of gardens.
We will show how he died, your ghost:
where the sunflower nodded in perpetuity,
where a root slept, and a tree
burnt in the sunlight; where a heart stopped.
I, too, will be nervous
as I approach the sleeper
and the ear, that cauldron of suspicion,
fluting inward and mirroring the labyrinth
of the soul. We will do it so the king
will recognize himself,
even in the smoky light
of the tapers, and shudder. Observe!
If he twitches like a fly, or leaps up
in a flurry of gestures!
The torches will dim, if only for a moment,
silks will rustle and tapestries whisper
in the sudden, incandescent quiet.
Hair will bristle at the touch of horror.
We will remain still and let death
take its stance among the groundlings
of this rotten state.
Your father will hear

the oboes stop as the cries
of the guilty unearth him,
the last note lingering
on the liquid porches of the ear.
And the next time you see the ghost,
have him breathe on a mirror
and prove his shape. For death
is just the absence of time.
The rest is silence.

ADVICE

There are times when I would say:
put down your pen, rise
from your desk and just walk away.
Leave the wrack of strewn papers
and the open wings of books.
Leave the ropery of written language,
its infinite treacheries, its diabolical expositions.
Leave Grushenka sulking at dawn
by the banks of the indifferent Volga.
Accept that realism is over-rated,
that plot is an elaborate joke. Abandon
literature's dead-ends of grief
and quatrains of the inexplicable.
Instead, build a stone wall, stack firewood,
sweep the stairs, star-gaze. Do anything
but write. Walk, clothed in rags,
into the astonishing world. Walk
into shadow, and the hollows of shadow.
Consider the lost river of your life.
Know that a stroke of lightning
may not be enough. Shudder
with disappointment.
Refuse to say it all. Be alone.
Ignore deadlines. Fish.

WINTER CROWS

They are impatient, pacing
in their silken topcoats,
and eyeing the snowfield
picked clean as a martyr's skull.

They've spent the brief winter day
discussing Lizzie Borden's funeral
arrangements, and now it is darkening.
But in July, the green corn

will be endless, and there will be but one
mad painter, with only one ear left,
to hear their wings
scythe the air.

LINES SCRAWLED IN THE DARK

A broken wristwatch hangs from a bent nail.
I press on a book and it disappears.
The night is a windy crossroads.
The trees are rustling
as if trying to speak. The leaves
enter their towers. I can hear chalk
on a blackboard somewhere
in a dark schoolroom
with a broken window.

THE FOG OF SAN FRANCISCO

For Bob and Regina

The fog of San Francisco is not your pea soup fog

    nor the pernicious steams

            of the London particulars

It is not the brine spiked mists of New England

        nor Seattle's dripping

    shrouds

It is not the Gothic dove gray brumes of Paris

      but an unearthly fog

        a spectral sea driven fog that pours

          down narrow streets with the breath of

  the sea

      rolling over the hills

        of Russian Protrero Telegraph and Nob

        flowing through the secret

neon alleyways of Chinatown

    drowning the longshoremen's saloons of North Beach

        and thrumming the bridge and its golden cables

      until even the towns of the peninsula and East Bay

flicker like sea glass in the gloom

and fog horn shadows sweep

over still, dark islands

where oyster beds slumber beneath

blankets of fog

Then San Francisco becomes a place lost in fog light

and seems to float above the world

until the dawn takes it back once again

with the morning light

DREAM

I pursue you through the crowded streets
of another bitter city, arms numb
to the wrists, reaching for you across
the silence between us.

Your red hair grown long again,
flaming back over your gray coat.
Wet leaves surround your face,
your footprints scattered.

I call to you over and over
as you sink into the flickering
weather of faces, your face falling
like a stone through deep water.

And when you finally turn to me,
you're just a woman in a long gray coat
whose name I no longer know.

THE INSOMNIAC'S MONOLOGUE

I can't sleep.
But you know that already.
Instead, I lie awake
on a bed of nails, one ear swaddled
in the pillow's cauldron,
tossing in razor grass.
The world has stopped.
It listens to my heartbeat
in the impenetrable, hangman's quiet.
The clock nails down the hatch
on another minute, the gate slammed
shut on another opportunity
now consigned to someone
more deserving. The digits are bright
splinters of time, green as lichen
on night's mute wall. Mice
scratch in the puzzle of night.
How fragile the world, how tiny.
How flat sleep's tundra,
and without landmarks.
Nothing near or far,
but somewhere a grave is being prepared.
Somewhere, there is a fork in the night,
a place where the path divides
and a choice must be made.
I have never reached that place.
Instead, I am trying to sleep
as night erodes, leaving only another dawn,
and the light that will once again illumine
an inexplicable city.

PRAISE FOR MY OYSTER KNIFE

Horn and tooth, weapon and tool,
the stainless knife blazes with a crow's
smile, twists round to north,

toward the mouth
of the nearest oyster,
its thirst assuaged solely

by the unholy blood of a stone.
Steel against bone,
the knife finds its place

at the stubborn hinge—
the notch behind the ear—
and plunges forth.

The edges of the shell
fly apart revealing a secret world
that accepts the knife,

accepts the smile.

THE LAST DAY OF THE WORLD

Already, on isolated farms, men
dazed by a sudden frost
are herding their ghost cattle.

A fisherman sitting by a brook,
inspects the scar from a childhood wound
as the deep ear of the water unfurls.

The farrier, too, sits alone
the bellows held loosely in his hands
like a divining rod.

The owl's deep questions patrol the marsh
as they always have. The hawthorn
and the ash, under all that cloud,
are still inscrutable.

There is no prophet,
no oracle to herald with silence
the cool rim of the world breeding thunder,
rain flickering on the last rose.

FISHERMAN

—for Joe Kilgallen

Your lake is quiet now.
Not even the geese darken its plain
as the pike, the old ones,
wait for you in their deep shoals.

I remember nights we fished there together,
drifting and casting under trees
that blossomed heavily in the dark
in the hope that a lunker might rise.

And I want to tell you, Joe
that the branch of the dogwood
still flowers, that the nets
of the fishermen still glisten.

And I remember once, I watched you,
where the blueberry thickets bent deep,
wading the shallows and gathering berries
and the shadows of berries.

BLISS

Tomatoes cool themselves
in the long breezes,
hoarding in their flesh
fabulous waters.

In the dry season, they are red cups
drinking summer light.

Late August, they grow lustrous,
dense in wild clusters.

I have come for them
with a basket and a knife,
my thirst ripened.

Picked, they shine in my hand
like wet stones, their skin like ours
burnished after love.

AVOCADO

An avocado rests
on the kitchen windowsill,

a luxurious carriage of green light,
globe and oblong moon of spring.

Indecipherable runes ripple the dark skin
as though it had passed through fire,

and set in the jade of its pale flesh,
the dark brown nut like rubbed mahogany.

Take a long knife and cut the avocado
in two. Cradle it in your two hands.

The odor is slightly musty, like an old well
where the five senses have come to drink and drowse.

THE WOLVES

The wolves howl because the rivers
have frozen, because under moonlight
the plains are endless
and the silk roads and caravan routes

are no longer traveled
by those boreal marauders in thick furs
whose mounts once churned the snow
of moon-bound steppes.

The animals have learned to avoid us
and we live now in the dark,
all directions the same: elsewhere.
No longer served by weapons,

we listen to wolves at night
as another squall lengthens our vigil
and stars fail.

FLYING AT NIGHT

I love flying at night
when the cabin goes dark
and passengers settle in
for the long flight, hunched

with books under their solitary
lamps, or huddled under overcoats,
sleeping in the engine's deep hum.
Then you can look out the window

at the crescent moon slung like a deer's rib
in the black sky, or down at the lights
of tiny towns blowing like sparks
across the darkened plains.

Part III

OCTOBER

Down the yellow street
unlit pumpkins
bear their masks.

PRAISE FOR BLACK COFFEE

Brew me cowboy coffee, boiled
over a mesquite fire, an egg—yoke
and shell—tossed in to sink the grounds

like ore, one eye on the pre-dawn star,
the other squinting against the smoke.
Give me the ink-dark java of those who

pull watch on sea-going freighters,
the typesetter who pours over his leaden
glyphs at 4:00 am. I long for the smoky,

bituminous espressos of the Mediterranean,
or Viennese—the dense, meditative brew
of the firebrand and the pamphleteer. I crave

Arabica, high and airy, smoky Kenyan or earthen
Guatemalan: pods charred to voltage then ground
to dust by the weight of the world; one sip

and you quiver like an apiary. Pour me
the rough coffee of shepherds, brewed
over a turf fire as autumn stars plunge

behind the hills. And at the end of the trail,
I want a tin cup of joe largely qualified
with a slug of whisky. And as I hunch

over my piping mug, steam rising like gratitude,
I'll spend the hours considering my options,
no other tasks before me but liberating

the proletariat or once again watching dawn
rip through the rim of another day
just like this one.

THE PRODIGY'S MONOLOGUE

In countless gambits, I sacrificed
legions of pawns on the bitter geometry
of the chessboard. My blind uncle had taught me.
He was a Prussian, an officer in the Great War
who'd learned chess in the trenches.
As a child, the checkered kitchen floor
was my field where I played at war
with tiny lead soldiers, each square
a country poised for capture—
obsidian, zones of startling pearl.
I loved their purity, the severity,
and insoluble arithmetic of crossroads.
I loved their rigors and disappointments.
I learned cartography and astronomy,
cosmology and metaphysics, wisdom
from my opponents, and humility
from those I routed. As a young man,
I studied military history, sprawled
with the board on a scarlet rug.
The ebony pieces glowered in the firelight,
the alabaster flaring like phosphorus.
I came to know the game clock's terror.
I plotted ambuscades and flanking tactics,
learned to yield and sacrifice and to perish.
By age seven, nothing frightened me.
I swept pawns to the end
of the immaculate and perfect board,
the landscape of my uncounted dead.
From the turrets of a rook,
I listened to withering silences,
across a landscape where pawns
were extinguished in anonymity.
One day, I will retire
and live in the tall, fierce tower,
climb its cool, dark stairs
and survey the lands I have conquered:
Gaul and Persia, Phoenicia, Germania,

and Troy. The bishop will pronounce us
Master and Queen, and I will take you
up the white rook's ivory stairs
to see at last the edge of
a ruined world.

WINTER MAILBOXES

They lean into the wind
these Quonset huts of silence,
satellites of winter's news

tilting on their bare axes
and shuddering on a decaying orbit
of light. Countless snows

have blasted them, winter rains
pound their rattling armatures.
The battered doors creak on rusted

latches, and the moon is a chalk mark
in the black sky as you reach
into that vast, echoing cavern

for the circulars, the dead letters,
for the late evening news and mail.

EIGHT SHORT POEMS ON THE HUMAN SHADOW

It will go where you're going,
and be there with you
at the end of your trip.
                    —Raymond Carver

1.
Squat on your heels
before an open fire.
On the ground behind you
your shadow quivers
with the memory
of grass fires.

2.
If I cup a hand to my ear,
it leans closer to hear
what I hear. Watches carefully
as I remove my hat, shade
my eyes and look
into the distance, or reach
for the tall flagon of a rose.
Watches everything I do
—the body's pupil.

3.
Noon: the day passes its tropic.
Picking blackberries
a shadow
crawls up your spine.

4.
Marvel quietly
at the silhouette
of a hanging man,
the uncertainties of a plum;
bats upside down in a tree.
Your shadow is an oracle.
It tells you where dark things

are hung, and of dark things coming.

5.
Its destination is my own: somewhere
else—a crossroads
moored to a post
from which the signs
have been torn away by the wind.

6.
On the long walk home,
red dust trails us
like a burning bird.
It pauses, waits
for me even as I stop
and bend to pick
a bee-wounded flower.

7.
Pinned to the wall
like a butterfly, its wings
make small dark
angels in the dying light.

8.
One day, it will be a scarecrow
waiting for you at the end
of a road. You turn
and walk away, feeling
its eyes on your back.
There is a crow on its shoulder,
and its cry is your own.

THE GRAVEDIGGER'S MONOLOGUE

Well, it's the Prince of Peeves,
back for the festivities
with that murder-of-crows
look, about as funny as a thumb-screw.
You never truly knew anybody,
fat boy, well or otherwise.
At the first smell of ambition
you turn tail and run like a thief.
You think that business
in England was clever? Wait til you see
what they harrow up for you
in rotten old Denmark.
It's no grand piano believe me,
Prince, you beekeeper.
Talk about skullduggery.
What do you know of it?
Wait until you haven't got a leg
to stand on. I'll enjoy a Woodbine in Hell,
before you, you emblematic wolf-mutt,
ever cipher this out. And if you ask me
whose grave I'm up to my pizzle
in why of course it's anyone's but mine.
So think about it. Grave matters, indeed.
Tell that to the fair Ophelia who, I've heard,
hath had too much. This is my universe,
the hammer and tongs, the dented flagons,
the verdigris, toe of peasant, heel
of courtier, the whole ball of wax.
Like I said, grave matters all. But
eventually, I'll climb out, while the rest of you
have only the getting in to look forward to,
for there is no future but the grave.
I've choked on the putrefaction,
the indignity of it. While you capered,
gamboled and cajoled. I've sliced down
deep where the shale lies,
cracked hands on the bare haft

of the only shovel in Denmark,
thrown spadefuls of dirt over my
naked shoulder onto the white shoes
of the Bishop. It's not the unknown soldier
I exhume, nor your whoreson moldering
father. Watch now as I haul this knave up.
Go ahead: lift the vacant skull, announce
its familiarity. Behold the ruined chops
of the jester—a stand-up comic no more.
Better get used to it, laddie. Mull the firmament
cupped there in the skull's vacuous luminescence,
planetary and blue.

CHOOSING A STONE II

Every stone tells a story.
I'm sure of it. Lay your head
against a stone. Listen

as it utters its histories:
how it once ground an axe,
marked the grave of a child,

traveled miles in the boot
of a soldier retreating
from Moscow, then sunk

into the muck of a river
like a star. Water flows
around it, pouring

over its inscrutable armature,
the stone bowing in supplication.
(That's the way it is with stones.)

Every stone tells a story.
Yours is still out there,
waiting for you. Choose a stone

but by evening leave it at the bend
in the road to mark the place
where you got lost,

or drop it into your pocket
for luck if nothing else.

MID-WINTER VIGIL

The wind smells like nails.
In the North, clouds

lower their heavy kettles.
The sky is chalk, the roads

carbon; their salts abrade.
Light glances off snow. Sound

travels farther over ice. Numb
to the wrists the copper beeches

retreat into their cells. Sparrows
squall and scatter across the snow

where the wind scrawls its wild name.
The jawbone of the moon drops

as the hourglass scuttles its grains.

TOURISTS: YORK HARBOR, MAINE

Season after season, I sit on the porch and watch
them as they roll into this cramped lobster town

in land yachts getting six miles to the gallon, the parade
from New Jersey and New York, Delaware, Virginia,

Florida—places where they apparently can no longer
find their own coastlines even in states like Rhode Island.

They're on vacation and resolutely hauling their earnest
gear to the edge of the implacable Atlantic in the chill

of a Maine summer, under a pewter sky where the shrill
protestations of gulls echo over the unforgiving slate

of the sea. They could be asleep in hammocks, golfing,
gardening or attending a baseball game somewhere

on the congenial plains of the Midwest or among the
sunblanched stadia of Colorado or Arizona—green fields

bright as a sundial. But there they go, in sandals
and straw hats, descending to this tough, thin strip

of crushed granite where terse swirls of fog dampen
the air, following the unspoken imperative to have fun

at the beach, carrying bright plastic buckets
and collapsible chairs under their arms.

TELEVISION I

Late at night, when the channels finally go off the air, bog water fills the circuits and the angered technicians are out on country roads checking the lines for trouble. In your living room, the panicked cables have stopped coming in and the screen is clogged once again with the dust of the sea. Once more, the television is just a stone blinking into heavy rain. Suddenly the whole room flares in the drizzle. The television snares whatever animals haven't yet climbed trees, apologizes to whoever is still hiding under the bed, and calmly nails your nightmares like a coin to the mast of a ship in an electrical storm. The Arctic and sub-Arctic continents are ablaze. I could go on but it's raining on the TV now, the static raining like a plague. Try now to switch off the tube and jump into bed before the snow starts falling.

SUMMIT

When we abandoned
the cylinders a blue flame
lit the ice. The flap of the

rucksack snapped
in the harsh wind. The thin air
made it hard to think.

We couldn't find our shadows.
Our Sherpa lost the power of speech.
We grew older by the second.

Climbing together, tethered
by the wind, Cragenauer
thought he could see

all the way into the Raj, and across
to the flat green plains
and lush terraces of the Assam.

Our stories dwindled. An ice ax
arrested my ascent.
We kicked some more holes

in the wind, in the green glaciers.
Then our radio was torn out of my hand,
gusts ripping our bodies

like prayer flags. The knots were
deafening, then silenced by ice. Then
snapped, stretching as they were

to the ends of the earth.

MUMMIES

—Milwaukee Public Museum

When children ask if it's frightening
when they come alive, I tell them yes,
of course it is, it's absolutely terrifying,
and believe me, you don't want to be around

when it happens, especially at night.
When they ask if the mummies walk
with their arms outstretched like mummies
in the movies, I tell them no, it's nothing

like that. You see, I explain, the muscles
of their arms have atrophied from thousands
of years of disuse; they just can't walk
around the way mummies do in movies.

In fact, I explain, their feet have been so
lovingly and carefully bound by strips
of linen, that it's difficult for them
to walk at all which explains the halting

gate, the fear that at any moment they will stumble
and pitch forward, landing in a heap of rags.
Can they talk? No, they can't talk, not after
all those years in tombs choked with the dust

of centuries and the weight of eternity
upon them. Can they see, they want to know.
Not any more, I say, for their eyes
were replaced with onions or stones,

stones as white as the sun. Finally, I explain,
they long only to wander forth as they used to,
so long ago and once again admire their reflections
in the shimmering Nile of the gallery floor.

ODE TO THE HUMAN SHOULDER

It is the flying buttress of the body,
transforming shirt or coat into architecture.
It is the body's fabulous rampart
from which a small child takes in
the expanse of the world. The blunt,
dense brow of the torso—
obtuse, obdurate, self-effacing—
it is nonetheless capable of an astonishing range
and subtlety of expression: the seductive flex
and lift of the come hither, a shrug
of resignation, impunity or indifference.
In defeat they are slumped, or in victory
hoisted in a flash of pride. In the bestiary
of the body it is the ox, the bull, the draft horse,
assuming both those spiritual and temporal
burdens unsuited to the slight and delicate birds
of the hands. Carpenter's square, shipwright's tool,
battering ram splintering locked doors
in a fit of passion, the shoulder retains
a bewildering seductiveness and guile,
allowing an evening gown to descend
like tapestry, revealing the shoulders
like new moons and cupping the airy shadow
at the clavicle. Rarely erotic
until just slightly revealed, its relation
to the rest of the body is subtle and infinite
echoing the bent knee, crooked elbow,
delicious arc of buttock or hip
and suggesting the body's numerous frontiers.
And then to descend: down the shadowy slope
of the back, down the spiral staircase
to where the harp-shaped blades
assert a beguiling prominence
reminding the bewitched observer
of a time when we had wings.

THE ART OF WRITING

I rearrange the paint cans, moving
the rustier ones to the back of the shelf,
check the opera schedule on the radio,
call the exterminator, look up used book stores

in our dog-eared yellow pages. Then
I'll study my fingernails awhile until
they glow with a cool, interplanetary light,
examining them as though an eclipse

might transpire across their slight
and imperfect moons. From there I move on
to the fingertips where the body
harbors its strange, translucent

labyrinths, then consider the hand itself
and imagine wandering, if I could, its 27 shining
ridges of bone, all to keep me from thinking
about what I really fear: the blank page,

how its emptiness is blinding like a terrible fever.
What I truly love is when it's over,
when the afternoon light
is behind me, the light that illumined

my hand hauling the pen across the trackless plains
of the paper desert. It is only then
that I emerge into the dying evening
light, nothing much on my mind,

heart weightless as a dragonfly, head
like a colander, admiring the spike weed,
the thunderheads.

TELEVISION II

Late summer. Another night alone, as I am on so many evenings, waiting for the end of the world. I know it's the end because I'm watching it on TV, the screen full of ghosts, and the television tuned to a channel exclusively broadcasting the news of earthquakes, insurrections, floods and mining disasters. I munch an apple as I watch the terrible news of the world unfold, its skin the color of flame, in its white flesh the immensity of the void the television has torn in the otherwise perfect darkness. Night draws closer, the TV screen glowing brighter with each report from the front, as with the bodies of electrocuted moths.

PRAYER TO A FUTURE DAUGHTER

Already, I count those snowbound nights
when I will be awake with you,
your lights coming on so slowly,
as we embrace and console each other
numbering together those dusty constellations

of the north. I believe in you, voyager
of the shadowy fathoms
that veil us from each other.

And I wonder what will bring you forth
to that place where I will divide
my flesh with you. When I have passed
great forests in silence, or passed
through the fire of the end of another day?

But I would tell you now, if I could,
not to be afraid, that the moon
is just a lost tooth, a childless gypsy
astray in the blue.

That one day your flesh will whiten
and grow dense as this dawn
that I hold now in my arms.

SLEEP

My face is always the first part to leave my body
and wander off into the heavy darkness.

All of its bones folding up, growing thin as needles
and leaving the rest of the body behind.

Perhaps I go about with no head,
leaving footprints as if it were snowing.

Then I understand what the violin strings
have been telling me, why the grasses grow
so long in summer.

How the grasses have been teaching the sky
to move in little steps.

WEDDING DAY

Rain blurred the windshield
as we drove north through a landscape
we'd never seen before, spring pastures

brimming in the evening light. And if, as they say,
rain is good luck on a wedding day, then we shall
be deluged with an embarrassment of fortune.

Love, let me sleep in the wipers' metronome
while you drive us through this new land
through which we pass like strangers.

THE LAST EXPLORER

My nails turn white in the bitter wind.
Feet thicken in the frost. Standing
just beyond the firelight, I can see
how the moon is an ax

grinding itself against the wind.
By dawn, I will turn into a spruce
standing at the edge of a snowbound forest
torn by the wind

and cradling an armload of blue needles.

ACKNOWLEDGMENTS

The author is grateful to the following magazines in which the poems from this manuscript previously appeared: *Alimentum*: "Basque Cooking"; *Amoskeag*: "A Cup of Tea"; *Arsenic Lobster*: "Coat of Arms" and "The Insomniac's Monologue"; *Chautauqua Literary Review*: "Horse Lessons" and "The Discovery of Heaven"; *Chicago Quarterly Review*: "Choosing s Stone II"; *Color Wheel*: "Birches"; *Cutbank*: "Sleep"; *DASH*: "The Last Explorer"; *Eclipse*: "Advice"; *Front Range Review*: "A Driftwood Fire in Winter", At Night", "Reading Yourself to Sleep"; *Having a Whiskey Coke with You*: "Dove," "Eight Short Poems on the Human Shadow"; *Kentucky Review*: "Flying at Night," Mid-Winter Vigil" and "Winter Mailboxes"; *The Kerf*: "Bliss"; *Kestrel*: "Praise for Black Coffee"; *The Midwest Quarterly*: "Television"; *Negative Capability*: "Ophelia"; *Off the Coast*: "Hammock Season"; *Pine Island Journal*: "The Invaders"; *The Puckerbrush Review*: "Fisherman"; *Rattle*: "Mummies"; *Red Owl*: "Navigator" and "The Wolves"; *Skald*: "Beowulf"; *South Dakota Review*: "Choosing a Stone I" and "The Last Day of the World"; *Steam Ticket*: "The Great Horned Owl's Monologue"; *Stolen Island Review*: "For a Shell Found on the Shore" and "Praise for My Oyster Knife"; *Verse Wisconsin*: "At the Vernal Equinox" and "Winter Crows."

"The Gravedigger's Monologue" appeared in the anthology, *Feast of Fools* (2010). "Ophelia" and "The First Player's Monologue" appeared in *In a Fine Frenzy—Poets Respond to Shakespeare (2005)*.
"Steelhead" appeared in *The Anthology of New England Writers* (1999).
"Mummies," appears in the textbook, *Into Reading, Volume 2*, published by Houghton Mifflin Harcourt, 2020.

Some of the poems in this manuscript appeared in a chapbook, *The Discovery of Heaven* (Parallel Press, 2006).

Born in Albany, NY, **Richard Hedderman** has worked as a housepainter, freelance writer, actor, voice-over artist, stage combat choreographer, and museum educator. A Pushcart-nominated (2017, 2019) poet and author, he taught English at Collège St. François-Xavier in Vannes, France, and earned degrees in English Literature and Theater at the University of San Francisco, and a MA in English/Creative Writing from the University of New Hampshire. He is the author of a chapbook, *The Discovery of Heaven* (Parallel Press), and his writing has appeared in dozens of literary publications both in the U.S. and abroad. Several of his poems and essays have been featured on public radio, and he appeared as a guest poet at the Library of Congress with the Poetry at Noon program. He serves on the Education staff at the Milwaukee Public Museum where he coordinates creative writing programming. He lives in Milwaukee with his wife, theatre professor and playwright Robin Mello.

www.ingramcontent.com/pod-product-compliance
Lightning Source LLC
Chambersburg PA
CBHW021155090426
42740CB00008B/1102